C000173211

Dolly Doctor

Pictures of Bygone Island Life

The Islands Book Trust

Published in 2009 by The Islands Book Trust

www.theislandsbooktrust.com

© The Islands Book Trust, 2009

ISBN: 978-0-9560764-1-0

Typeset by Two Ravens Press Ltd, Ullapool, Scotland
www.tworavenspress.com

The Islands Book Trust would like to thank the Lewis Museum Trust
for their assistance in the publication of this volume.

Printed on Forest Stewardship Council-accredited paper
by the MPG Books Group, Bodmin and King's Lynn

The Islands Book Trust
Ravenspoint Centre
Kershader
South Lochs
Isle of Lewis
HS2 9QA
Tel: 01851 820946

THE ISLANDS BOOK TRUST
URRAS LEABHRAICHEAN NAN EILEAN

Foreword

I am sure this volume of pictures from the photographic collection of Dr Donald MacDonald of Gisla (affectionately known as Dolly Doctor) will be of great interest to many people in the Outer Hebrides and further afield.

They recall vividly – perhaps more vividly than can words alone – a bygone way of island rural life from the first half of the twentieth century. During these years, customs such as the annual journey to the summer shielings, the swimming of cattle across the channel from Great Bernera, traditional methods of dying wool, bringing peats back to the croft from the moor in a creel, and living in a thatched 'black house', were still common-place – whereas today they are largely memories. It was Dolly Doctor's great good fortune, and achievement, to have witnessed such common-day practices, and to have had the foresight to have recorded them on camera.

I am very grateful to Peter Cunningham, who was a friend of Dr MacDonald, for writing an introduction, and also for preparing the informative captions to the photographs. In more recent years, Peter has attracted large audiences to his presentations of Dolly Doctor slides (including two for The Islands Book Trust in Stornoway and Uig, respectively), and it was the requests made at these meetings which were the genesis of this book. We are grateful for approval and financial support from the Trustees of the Lewis Museum to enable us to convert the idea of a permanent record of the slides into a reality.

A couple of other points should also be made at the outset:

1. In making this selection for publication, we have tried to identify pictures which were taken by or for Dolly Doctor, rather than other pictures in his collection which were derived from other sources. We gratefully acknowledge advice from Peter Cunningham, Finlay MacLeod, and Michael Robson, and others at the various showings of the slides, in this connection, although despite our best

endeavours there remains an element of doubt about the provenance of some of the pictures.

2. While Donnie Morrison has worked wonders in enhancing the quality of the images presented in this book, there are limits to how far modern technology can improve pictures which have inherent faults such as over-exposure or poor focus. It has to be said that, while Dolly Doctor was a great collector of stories and historical memorabilia of island life, he was not a particularly gifted photographer, and furthermore the slides we have were made from the original glass plates. The importance of this book lies not in its photographic excellence, but in the historical significance of the scenes he recorded.

Despite these caveats, the Book Trust is very pleased to publish this volume, and hopes that it will give pleasure and provide useful information to many people.

John Randall
Chairman
The Islands Book Trust
2009

Introduction

Dr Donald Macdonald ('Dolly Doctor') was born in Stornoway in 1891, the eldest son of John Macdonald of Carishader, Uig, and Annie Gillies of Shawbost. He was educated at the Nicolson Institute in Stornoway and graduated Master of Arts at Aberdeen University. After teaching for a time he returned to university and graduated M.B. Ch.B. at Edinburgh. In 1919, while an undergraduate, he met Emily Paul, a niece of Lord Leverhulme, in Uig Lodge, where they were guests. They were married in Leverhulme's home in Hampstead in 1923 and he practised in Stoke Newington until he retired in 1946. On their marriage Leverhulme had given them the estate of Uig where they spent their holidays, at first in Uig Lodge and then in a house they built at Gisla which they called Gisla Lodge. The cost of running the whole estate proved too much for them.

He became absorbed in the history and folklore of the Outer Hebrides and took and collected many photographs of the way of life of the people and of their environment. He began also to collect obsolescent implements and artifacts for a museum that he hoped to establish in the Castle Grounds in a translocated traditional black house. For this purpose he set up the Lewis and Harris Folk Museum Society of which the Procurator Fiscal, Colin Scott Mackenzie, became Chairman and I Secretary. A considerable sum of money was raised by public exhibitions of his photographs which were enclosed between three-inch square glass plates and were projected by what was once called a 'magic lantern', an ancient and cumbersome metal box which threw out more heat than light. I was persuaded by 'Dolly Doctor' to accompany him on these expeditions and to operate the infernal machine and in this way became very familiar with the photographs and their content. A selection of these for the benefit of a wider public is the purpose of this book.

When Dr Macdonald died in 1961 his collection and 198 photographs were transferred to the care of the Society and the latter converted to 35mm format for use with modern equipment.

They have not worn well but, with the help of Donnie Morrison of Pairc House, Habost, Lochs, they have been restored to almost pristine condition and are now contained on a CD. This CD together with the original slides, the 35mm conversions and a recorded commentary will be on permanent loan to the Museum nan Eilean.

Mrs Emily Macdonald published the stories her husband had collected in *Tales and Traditions of the Lews* in 1967. Her own *Twenty Years of Hebridean Memories* had been published in 1939 and both books have been invaluable in the composition of the enclosed text. Every effort has been made to identify the persons and places exhibited and the help of the kindly people of Uig in this connection is much appreciated.

In closing, I wish to thank John Randall and The Islands Book Trust for the opportunity to contribute to this memorial to a rather special Lewisman. One day 'Dolly Doctor' and I passed each other on opposite sides of Bayhead. I was clad in an old ex-army kilt. Across the breadth of the street he shouted "Why are you wearing the Mackenzie tartan?" He was that kind of man, larger than life and spared not his friends.

Peter Cunningham
Aros, Ravens Lane,
Laxdale, Isle of Lewis
2009

Dolly Doctor

Pictures of Bygone Island Life

Carloway Dun or Broch with Mrs Emily Macdonald and friend. This type of dry-stone structure is concentrated in the north-west Highlands, the Northern and Western Isles. This specimen is a little lower than its original height. The seven foot thick double walls supported two or three floors and a staircase where the inhabitants lived. The central courtyard, 24 feet in diameter, is entered by a low, narrow tunnel defended by hidden spearmen. The open top was closed with turf or thatched. Many brochs were built on prominent heights, others on natural or artificial islets on fresh-water lochs and approached by stepping stones. Little if anything is known of who built them or for what purpose. W.C. Mackenzie argues that they were essentially forts for the protection of the native population and of pre-Celtic origin. In his *Tales and Traditions of the Lews* Dr Macdonald writes that the Carloway Broch was built in the 4th Century by a Darg Mac Nu-Aran and tells the story of its partial destruction in the 17th century by the Macaulays of Uig led by Donald Cam, an intrepid warrior and progenitor of Lord Macaulay and others of that ilk.

Dr Macdonald with a group of Stornoway Sea Cadets and their Founder and Director, Canon Anderson Meaden, about 1935. The tall 3rd Cadet from the left was Murdo Nicolson, 46 Seaforth Road. None of the others has been identified.

The estuary of the Grimersta River at the head of East Loch Roag, a large sea loch that opens out into the Atlantic and has been used by ships of the Royal Navy as a refuge or fleet anchorage.

Grimersta Lodge. Built in 1861 by Sir James Matheson to house his angling guests, it is now owned by a syndicate of anglers who have exclusive access to the sporting rights over the large estate, in particular to the famous salmon fishing in the river and four fresh-water lochs. The bag of 54 salmon caught by one rod in one day in 1888 has not been exceeded.

The Seal Cave. When seal meat was a valued source of protein, many were caught in the Seal Cave, situated a few miles north of Gress on the east coast.

Bee-hive Hut. Dr Macdonald is seen here emerging from one
of a group of remarkable, ancient, corbelled dwellings on the
Morsgail moor. Others may be found near Cliasmol in Harris.
They are said to be about 4000 years old and may have been
inhabited for 3000 years.

Morsgail Lodge was built by James Matheson about 1850 for his bride, whose favourite refuge it became. After its sale by Lord Leverhulme in 1923 it had several owners until its destruction by fire. Rebuilt and refurbished in 2007 on its beautiful site by Morsgail Loch, the house has resumed its role as a sporting lodge.

The Gisla River. Flowing into Little Loch Roag this was once a productive little salmon and sea trout river but was dammed in the 1950s to provide power for a hydro-electric plant.

Gisla Lodge. Lord Leverhulme presented the district of Uig to his niece and Dr Macdonald when they were married in 1923. With the assistance of his younger brother, Balla, a house was built here in 1926 which they called Gisla Lodge and which became a favourite holiday home. It is still occupied by Mrs Carol Macdonald, Balla's widow.

Baile na Cille Church of Scotland was erected in 1830 by the
Seaforth family to seat 1000 in response to a request by the Rev
Alexander Macleod, who came in 1824, the first evangelical
minister in Lewis. He had to preach in the open air on account
of the ruinous state of the old church by the graveyard. It is
now no longer in use.

Baile na Cille manse is now an hotel. The associated grave yard is connected with *Coinneach Odhar*, the Brahan Seer. In his *Tales and Traditions of the Lews* Dr Macdonald tells of Kenneth's discovery on *Cnoc Eothail* of the pebble that enabled him to foretell the shape of things to come.

Meavaig farmhouse and Church. Meavaig is a corruption of the Old Norse *Mjo-vik*, a narrow bay, and it is a very appropriate name, for this attractive village is tucked away at the head of a little inlet of Loch Roag. The first post office for the district was established here by 1880.

A general view of Valtos and Kneep. Valtos was given a pier in 1824 as it was already a fishing station and a salt store. At the time this photograph was taken there would have been five schools within the catchment area of the present Uig School. One was here at Valtos with 32 pupils and others at Loch Croistean with 47, Crowlista with 24, Mangersta with 18, and Islivig with 32, with an aggregate attendance in 1935, of 153 pupils. The present Uig School has 24 pupils. There were also side schools in the area at Aird Bheag/Hamnaway, Scaliscro, Morsgail, and Crola.

The Forsa river flows into Camus Uig from Loch Stacsabhat, through which salmon and sea trout pass into Loch Suaineabhat in substantial numbers, except during the fishing season when they are confined to Stacsabhat. The sporting rights are held by the owners of Uig Lodge.

This photograph of the spectacular gorge on the Forsa river was taken from the main road. A pair of ravens once nested on the cliff on the left bank.

Forsa Gorge. The pool below the falls is a notable holding pool for salmon but is almost impossible to fish properly.

Loch Stacsabhat below the 429m Suaineabhal. Black-throated Divers once nested on the island. Arthur Ransome stayed in Uig Lodge where he wrote *Great Northern Diver* and designed the popular salmon fly *Blue Elver,* using feathers of the South African Helmeted Guineafowl, *Numida meleagris.*

Aird Uig is a bleak, granitic headland whither crofters moved to
avoid emigration. An early warning radar station was erected
upon it during the 'Cold War', the ruins of which still litter the
place. A popular hotel and restaurant has been established here.

Camus Uig or Traighe Uige, a spacious, shallow bay, dominated by Uig Lodge, another of the Mathesons' sporting lodges, the view from whose windows changes hourly as the tide comes and goes. The Uig Chessmen were found in 1831 in the sand dunes at Ardroil, on the west side of the bay.

A black house on hillside above Little Loch Roag.

Dr Macdonald with Ronnie Maclean, a baker in Point Street in Stornoway, at the Red River *(Abhainn Caslabhat)*.

Historian W.C. Mackenzie (*History of the Outer Hebrides* 1903 and *The Book of the Lews* 1919 etc) with Captain Ruari Macleod of *S.S. Esperance Bay* on Loch Mor Coirgavat (?).

Dr Macdonald fishing Gisla river prior to erection of a dam at its exit from Loch Mor Coirgavat to supply a hydro-electric power station at its mouth.

Dr Macdonald with salmon. Wild Hebridean salmon aver-
aged 5 to 6 lbs., prior to pollution of the stock of wild fish by
escaped farmed fish.

Dr Macdonald with salmon and friend on the Old Mill Pool.

Dr Macdonald with sea trout. Such a catch is unlikely now
owing to the scarcity of their prey, sand eels, from over-fishing
and, possibly, global warming.

Macdonald with catch of finnock (immature sea trout)

Dr Macdonald on Loch Gruineabhat. This is a large fresh-water loch, some 3 miles west of Gisla and may be confused in some of the photographs with Loch Mor Coirgavat, owing to lack of information.

Ronnie Maclean with catch of brown trout
on Loch Mor Coirgavat.

John Maclean of 12 Crowlista, his daughter, Jessie, and his nephew, Peter Angus Maclean, 8 Timsgarry, driving cattle to shieling near Morsgail. This photograph was taken by Dr Macdonald from a window in the Lodge about 1935. This was the last time Crowlista cattle were taken to the shieling as the village grazings were later fenced.

Valtos men going to the shieling from Gisla. Angus Macaulay
stands in front of the mast; top right is John Morrison (Slim),
and in front of him is John Buchanan (Charraic).

A shieling is a primitive dry-stone, single roomed dwelling, set often in a remote part of the moor by standing or running water, in which the young women lived in summer who looked after the village cattle in order to rest the village grazings. They seldom lacked male company during the long summer evenings as many a romantic Gaelic song tells. All that remains of them now is a ruckle of stones in a bright green patch amongst the heather. The Gaelic name is *Àiridh*.

Murdo Buchanan, 18 Uigen, (Gladstone), Donald Buchanan, 9 Reef, and Angus Buchanan, 18 Uigen (Mogors), at Gisla, returning from a fank (sheepfold) with fleeces.

Visitors at a shieling.

Stock for Little Bernera at Bosta on Great Bernera. The former is a small, fertile island separated from Great Bernera by a narrow tide-swept channel. The ruins of a pre-Reformation chapel lie in a graveyard on the south-east corner.

Valtos men arriving at Gisla with gear and supplies for a shieling,
which was re-thatched annually.

Calum Buchanan, 7 Valtos, and Murdo Smith, 30 Valtos, at Gisla, returning from fank with fleeces.

Swimming cattle across the sound from Great Bernera to
Earshader. Women were taken across first in order to call the
cattle to them. A bridge now spans this turbulent channel.

Swimming cattle. As long as the beasts' heads were kept above water they survived the change of element.

Swimming cattle. Boat at anchor is said to have been last *Zulu* in use in Great Bernera. This type of open fishing vessel was first developed in Lossiemouth in 1879, the year the Zulu War broke out, and became popular on the west coast. Up to 80 feet in length it was carvel built with an upright straight stem and raked stern. The *Muirneag* was the last working *Zulu* in Lewis.

Valtos crofters on their way to shearing at *Bothan Ruadh* at the head of Loch Suaineabhat. Kenny Mackay's van in background. When, one wonders, was the first road vehicle brought to Stornoway?

A fank at Bosta. The district graveyard lies here behind an Iron Age village and a popular sandy beach looking out upon the islands of outer Loch Roag.

Spinning yarn. The wheels introduced by Mrs Stewart Mackenzie about 1830 were large 'muckle' wheels. They were replaced
by smaller, transverse wheels that were not popular. The present
wheel is said to have been brought by East Coast fishermen
and it was when the late Archie Macrae, Keith Street, began
to make them that they became popular.

Woman with spinning wheel.

John Macritchie gathering crotal for the dyeing of wool.

John Macritchie dying wool in an old tar drum.

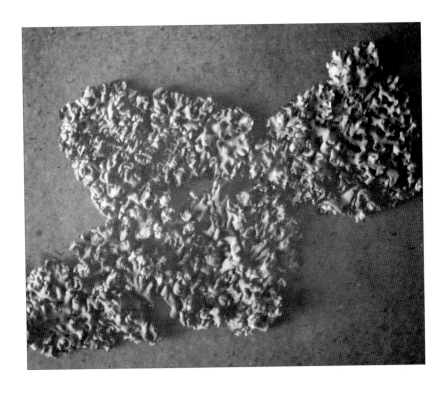

Crotal is a common lichen of the genus *Parmelia* found on rocky surfaces. It dyes wool a rich brown and was in common use with Harris Tweed. A black dye was derived from peat soot, water lilies or poison ivy, yellow from sorrel or ragwort (if copper coins were added to the ragwort a more coppery colour was produced). Shades of grey to green were got from iris roots and mussel shells.

Dyed wool being dried.

John Gillies weaving on a primitive wooden handloom. This type of loom was replaced by the Hattersley loom which was introduced by Lord Leverhulme.

Waulking tweed; a process carried out by women to shrink the fabric, to the rhythmical strain of traditional or extempore, and sometimes ribald, songs.

Duncan Maclean with finished Harris Tweed. It was the
Countess of Dunmore who, about 1844, created a market
for the home-made tweed amongst her friends in the south
of England and encouraged her tenants in Harris to produce
tweed for sale. By 1881 the merchants in Stornoway had begun
to profit from their enterprise, mechanised the preparation of
yarn and the finishing processes in new mills and in the 1960s
were producing seven million yards a year of what was by then
called 'Harris' Tweed.

Cutting peat with *tairisgeir*. This is a peat-spade made usually by the local blacksmith and wielded by the upper of two persons while the lower one throws the cut slab of peat up on to the bank to dry. Bona fide crofters have an inalienable right from time immemorial to cut an agreed amount of peat on the common grazings. Residents in the Stornoway Estate must pay a nominal fee for the privilege.

Bare-footed woman with peat creel. Shoes were seldom worn except, for example, on Sundays. Folk visiting Stornoway from the Lochs area came bare-footed across the moor to the burn at Bayhead where they washed their feet and shod themselves. The burn is still called *Allt nam Bròg* (Shoe Burn).

Peat creel. Creels were usually home-made from willow grown in a dry-stone enclosure on the croft called *lios*.

Cut peat undergoing final drying after some weeks drying on banks. Traditionally, freshly cut peats were laid flat on heather for three weeks, after which three or four were piled on edge together in *ruthain* for two weeks when they were gathered into *ath-ruthain,* as in this photograph.

A typical peat bank. The formation of peat in Lewis began in the Atlantic period, about 6,500 years ago, when mild, wet conditions favoured its growth. Mosses, lichens and vascular plants slowly colonised the ice-polished, impervious gneiss and as they decayed were compressed by succeeding deposits in anaerobic conditions into what we call peat. It may be therefore that the lowest layer of peat was laid down before the Lord told Abram to leave Ur of the Chaldees.

Dolina Macdonald going for peats. In former times the dried peat was brought in this way from the moor as required. When an enterprising member of the community acquired a road vehicle, such as a tipping lorry, he was employed to bring home comparatively immense loads carefully stacked to survive the rough ride back. The arrival of the tractor and trailer made peat banks distant from the road available.

Murdag with full creel. The burden of cutting and storing of peat was, like other annual crofting tasks, lambing, dipping, shearing, harvesting and fishing, shared by the extended family and neighbours and was so lightened as to become a joyous occasion for gossip and discourse.

Angus Smith, Carishader, with pet lamb.

A Crofter family. Overcrowding during the late 19th and early
20th centuries hastened the spread in Lewis of tuberculosis
(Tinneas caitheamh), the greatest single killer disease in Lewis.
It was not until the advent of new drugs in the 1950s, improved
housing conditions and education enabled the Medical Officer
of Health in Lewis, Dr R.S. Doig, to overcome this wasting
illness.

A Crofter family in Carloway. As the Hebridean crofter family was a closely knit unit, so the extended family and, indeed, the whole township were deeply sensitive to the cares and needs of their members. In 1976 Angus Maciver, a young bachelor living alone at 32 Knock Carloway, was found to have kidney failure, formerly a fatal disease. The Carloway people began to raise funds for a home dialysis unit and, within two weeks, £5000 had been raised, amounting finally to £23000 from resident and exiled Lewis people. The Carloway water was found to be unsuitable but, with help from the National Health Service, a unit was established in Lewis Hospital and later in Carloway, in which Angus was devotedly cared for by his two sisters.

Mrs Anne Macneil, 11 Carishader, with Seonag, Anne and Dolag. The girls' hair was probably cut short owing to infectious illness such as measles.

John Gillies, 9 Carishader, and his wife. As can be seen here, the roads through Uig were narrow and unpaved, meant only for pedestrians and horse and cart. In 1844 there were 44 miles of road in Lewis. During his tenure of the island Sir James Matheson added 154 together with bridges. Not bad when one considers the tools and equipment available. Even by the 1950s part of the link between Carloway and Shawbost at Dalbeg was unsurfaced. Tarmacadam was developed about 1820 by John Loudon McAdam but obviously took some time to arrive in Lewis.

Family outside black house. By children such as these, education was hard won. There was a time when in summer, on bare feet and by rough roads and paths, they made their way to a small school, perhaps carrying a peat for the classroom fire, expecting no food at mid-day until they got home again but for what food could be brought from home. Yet, the vital spark was there in some, nurtured by inspired and dedicated teachers, and they became administrators, captains of commerce and industry, leaders of men and scholars.

A black house. "The distinguishing feature of the Long Island black house was the exposed, broad, flat ledge extending round the house, the roof- couples rising from the inside of the wall, owing to the shortage of timber, other than flotsam. The wall itself was six feet thick, comprising two dry-stone walls two feet apart, infilled with earth and gravel. The floor was of beaten earth and the fire was on a stone slab in the middle of the living room, a hole in the roof serving as a chimney." (*Thatched Houses* Dr Colin Sinclair)

A ruined black house.

Roof of black house showing structure.

Borve Lodge, Harris. Built by Lord Dunmore in 1870, it was taken over by Lord Leverhulme, who built an elegant circular garden 1924, in which he installed a sophisticated sundial he brought from Lews Castle. It is a heliochronometer made by Pilkington Gibbs about 1913 and is one of only 1000 produced.

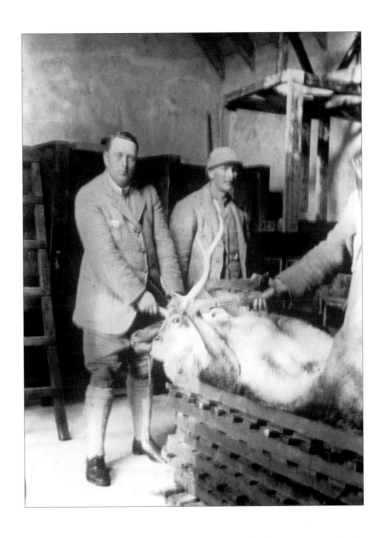

Macdonald with stag in the outside game larder at Borve Lodge.

In 1862 Charles Murray, the 7th Earl of Dunmore, who had bought Harris in 1834, built Ardvourlie Castle in a dark corner of Loch Seaforth in 1862. The Countess, formerly Lady Gertrude Coke, daughter of the 2nd Earl of Leicester, didn't like it, so three years later he built Amhuinnsuidhe Castle ("riverside seat") on a sunny site on the north shore of West Loch Tarbert. It was occupied by successive sporting tenants, including Sir Thomas Sopwith. Sir James Barrie took it for the 1912 season and conceived the famous play *Mary Rose*, set on Loch Vosmid nearby. His guests included fellow authors such as Anthony Hope, E.V. Lucas and A.E.W. Mason. In 2003 the North Harris Estate was bought out jointly by the residents and Ian Scarr-Hall. The castle is now a prodigious venue for house parties and for angling and deer stalking.

Salmon leap in front of Amhuinnsuidhe Castle. It provides a memorable spectacle when a shoal of fish enters the river from the sea.

Finsbay Lodge was built in 1903 by an association of anglers on the mainland to exploit the outstanding sea trout fishing on local lochs. It was eventually abandoned and the ruins removed by Lord Leverhulme. Michael Gardner wrote a valuable account of its history in 2008.

Clach Mhicleoid. A standing stone of unknown provenance,
similar to that at Balantrushal in Lewis.

Lord Leverhulme tried to set up a sea-fishing and processing industry at Obbe on the Sound of Harris when his plans for Lewis fell through. Here the present pier is being constructed at what was later called Leverburgh.

St Clement's Church, Rodel. Built about 1500 by the Macleods of Dunvegan and Harris. Rebuilt in 1784 by Captain Alexander Macleod and restored by the Countess of Dunmore in 1873. Now in the care of Historic Scotland.

Baptismal Font in St Clement's Church at Rodel.

Rodel Hotel was built in 1781 as a private house and had become an hotel by 1925. It was restored in 2003.

Sir Norman Macleod's house in Berneray (1614-1705). He was a famous scholar and fought in the Royalist army at the Battle of Worcester in 1651. He owned Berneray.

Sign above the door of Sir Norman Macleod's house in Berneray.

Barpa Langass. A chambered cairn on south side of A867
between Lochmaddy and Clachan in North Uist, erected as a
memorial to illustrious dead.

Barpa Langass. Person on left is Mrs Emily Macdonald.

Trinity Temple at Carinish, North Uist, is the most famous ecclesiastical building in North Uist, dating from early twelfth century and claimed to be the oldest university in Scotland. It was founded by Beathag, the daughter of Somerled and first prioress of Iona from 1203.

Trinity Temple. It was destroyed at the Reformation and is in a dangerous and scandalous state of dilapidation.

The grave at Balranald, North Uist, of the renowned Gaelic poet, Iain MacCodrum (1693-1779).

Dr D.J. Macleod, HM Inspector of Schools, crossing the North Ford from North Uist to Benbecula with Aonghas Cuagach, coachman at Creagorry Hotel, Benbecula.

North Ford. The landing place on Benbecula.

Cattle cooling off in North Ford.

Uist peat stack.

Pony with panniers. Unique in the Outer Hebrides, perhaps,
to the Uists and Barra.

Cathie Dunlop (?) with young Great Black-backed Gulls on an island on Loch Mor Coirgavat (?) near Gisla.

Hooded Crows on nest on an island on Loch Mor Coirgavat (?).

Herring Gulls' nest and eggs on an island on
Loch Mor Coirgavat (?).

Young Herring Gulls.

Red-throated Divers' nest and egg. This species is so made for flying and swimming rather than walking that it has to build its nest right at the water's edge of a lochan in order to be able to escape detection by diving from the nest into deep water.

Injured Gannet somewhere in Lewis. This species is unable to take off from a level surface unless in a gale.

Dr Donald Macdonald with Miss Kate Campbell outside her house at 17 Brue, Barvas. It is not known when or why this photograph was taken. It was possibly taken just before he died in 1961 and he might have been looking for a suitable, authentic black house to hold his collection or was, perhaps, just curious to examine one of the last surviving examples.